This Is Our Secret

Other works by Eric Williamson

Miscreant Issue Zero

This Is Our Secret

This Is Our Secret

chapbook series I

Eric Williamson

This Is Our Secret

Copyright 2023 © Eric Williamson, This Is Our Secret

Cover Design by NXOEED (James B. Hunt)

ISBN: 979-8-218-23255-9

CONTENTS

This Is Our Secret

MOMENTS

There is a couple arguing on the street corner

In plain daylight

In front of everyone

About neglect, about not fulfilling expectations

As a second couple walks past them holding hands

She looking up into his eye

He pulling her into a close embrace

And making it clear to everyone they are smitten

While the third couple spills out onto boulevard

From the small coffee shop

Laughing aloud for all to hear

While she giggles, he looks into the sky

MORNING CHILL

It was the world that was finally silent,

Water in a steel basin,

Placid, serene, and almost frozen.

The winter chill burned the windowpane with flares

Of hoarfrost, condensation, and memory

Of things lost, present, still breathing.

Her movement in the next room, returning to bed, was
  unsettling

A cabinet of china crashing to the floor,

And again, I knew she was loving me less.

Her dresser and bookshelf collected dust,

And above us, her dolls lined up like a firing line,

Picture frames, books, not having shifted for years,

Surrounded by dust circles built up like prison walls.

Insecurity hung in the air like her diaphanous canopy,

With the slightest hint of movement, I slid back in her.

She is not alone.

The morning was briefest minutes away

And her back was back kissing my nestled chest

While the alarm clock was spinning the same song.

If today was a new day, not the same as before,

If today was something new, where the chill

Didn't layer deceptive thoughts of need and warmth

If we are something different, not stuck in rote,

Then perhaps, our warmth might clear the frost,

Liquefy the chill from the trees, and set nature in motion

And of waterlilies, of geese flapping in glee,

Of a sunrise that scalds the flesh and emancipates

Our hearts from each other we might be.

IN THIS PLACE

where currency and blessings are not the same,

where tomorrow is less desire, more excuse,

a single wildflower

clutches her earth as if abandoned,

as if having suddenly become aware,

and having no way of sharing.

Feathers dust the roads.

Instead of capacious trees and skies,

the birds congregate in town halls

beneath parked cars.

In this place

seasons change

with ululations of sirens and buzzers,

flashing, whirling lights,

and not with lambent subtlety of shade and tone

that lets all know, just as a lover

slaps her lover's face for the first time,

that this is not the way it was intended to be.

In this place

a coyote

off Northern Ave.,

whose mordant disbelief

swallowed the city lights,

doesn't quite think the streets are the place to be,

saunters home with tail raised high

just in case someone had seen.

MOVING ON

These are such familiar settings to us both.

Dawn rising with mouths agape.

Just between the two of us,

come on, what is there left to say at a moment like this?

All our clothes coiled in copper wire

on thick plastic spools stacked in the front yard.

Your furniture, and what little is mine,

arranged in royal processional columns,

seashells with muffled voices,

candles half exposed,

statuettes, and yesterday's picture frames

outlined in dust on the window sills.

I'm dragging your antique love seat,

every inch channeling into the linoleum

with screams. Your pup's dust-bunnies scurry,

leaving me with chalk tongue, in this room.

I'm not crying. Not even when you

walk out to our mailbox on asphalt feet,

and descend to the stick-on address

with a razor and a smile. There is smoke.

I cough.

Wind touches your hair and then dies.

A haggard Lincoln chokes its final rebuke,

sputtering down the street. I always hated our neighbors.

I never knew them. That and the bullet hole

in the westernmost window of our home.

The U-haul squats in the gravel parkway,

long silver tongue-ramp licks the earth as I do my lips.

It swallows parcels as those sticker numbers curl

like metal shavings in your hand.

You're careful not to let any fall, collecting each digit

in a plastic bag

with a spoonful of gravel and spit.

I recall asking something about

giving,

while you are looking

up

through an olive tree at a cluster of twigs, dry leaves,

fragments. You never heard.

Moving into our bathroom, to the shower lining torn

from plastic rings in pops like gunfire, and fixtures scrubbed

with scent and fury and spine-scraping scratching,

the cabinets hollowed,

vulnerable and skinless; a fragile skeleton

shivering. You close the door. Turn off the light,

and yawn.

These "familiar settings." Our kitchen sink empty.

The pilot lights gagged.

A straw broom leaning into the corner,

chipped clay tile awaiting bare feet and my step,

in this room,

I stroke a cut on my lip with the back of my hand.

You enter, sigh, and place a hand on my shoulder,

a dirty rag on the counter,

your brow to my cheek, and outside the window

something darts up the fence

and is gone.

THEY ARE FOR NOW

Silence,

a sleepy moment

when little hearts

the way they are,

alone,

break.

She isn't laughing,

simply smiles,

her fingers curl

into her lips

like closing petals.

Her beauty

runs barefoot

ahead of her,

uncluttered,

shifting sand

beneath its weight.

There is a squall.

The surf breaks.

Voices rise unheard,

and the growing distance

between them

settles

into a shape

willing to contain.

Somewhere, bath water gets cold.

He stretches,

arches his back,

an incomplete bridge

dangling

from the end.

If he falls

fast enough

he may catch himself.

She holds his wrist

like smoke.

He pulls,

"Don't let go."

Tomorrow

on another island,

not quite unlike this,

2 children press palms

to lips, smack & wave.

A dozen black men

lower their fathers into holes

like mouths,

lifetimes spent

digging.

3 stars blink out.

1 changes from crimson

to honey.

WE STOLE THIS TIME TO TALK

We stole this time to talk, to repair

Resting our legs on the wrought iron park bench

Feet swaying in slow half circles like

Waves covering each other over on the beach

Streets seemed emptier than ever before

Debris collared inside the necks of nestled courtyards

She was my bird. Her arms flapping at her sides

Tightening and relaxing like a sail luffing in a gentle breeze

I kept my face as empty as I could, abandoned

Wiping the oil from beneath my eyes with my thumbs

Time had worked our bodies, she still a girl in respects

Marooned at the age when discovering habits was still a game

It was one of the traits loved at first

Then somewhere stopped loving, and now loved again

Far above a lamp had been lit behind the sky

Clouds slipped past as shadows moving slowly over grass

Birds followed a seam of wind soaring out of sight

Not waiting for the change in our world

We had simply closed our eyes one night

And woken one day in a room as strangers

Finally, she just gave up and said what I was thinking

"I didn't know you realized anything was wrong."

I gave the shallow, wincing laugh that people

Who don't admit a joke has embarrassed them give

The looks between us were older than time

Rotund bulges in the park knolls like graves

A child and mother nearby snacked on chips, fastidious

Like trying to split a seed open between front teeth

Months like shadows stretched out to meet the horizon

We, each day, collapsing at opposite ends of the couch

We talk, the night deepens, the sky soon all moon and stars

And we found ourselves the last people alive, wondering

Do we heal from the outside in or the inside out?

A body is more likely to die at sunset than any hour of the day

We are born with countless blessings

And do not realize they're blessings until they are lost

And sometimes we don't even realize they are lost

Until they come back

Rising from the park bench, we continued to talk

We touched fingertips; this was our time, not stolen

"You know," she said,

"That may be the best thing I've ever done with my life."

Or maybe it is chance

In the end, maybe it's nothing but chance

LATE NIGHT DRIVE

She will be blacked out,

a bombshell,

and won't say anything all the way home.

Her tender skin beaten and strewn,

highlighted and dog-eared, like a good text

or a lifetime commitment.

A little more is taken each day.

Her tears remain silent and clear.

This dawn recognizes his subtle disguise

in freckled skies.

The moon path only half discharged

and his lazy limbs arrest blood-stained eyes.

Higher and further out.

It's part of a cycle, this fading away,

a late-night drive inside.

His fist like liquid dynamite

wedged between her teeth,

like floss that snaps, minty and fresh...

She remembers: folded spring dried laundry

upon her knee and pressed panties to her lips,

dreams that scatter like dandelions on her breath,

like cockroaches in the kitchen's dark turned light,

that hides — in the cracks

the spaces between August and September.

The days are never meant to last as night

drives by her old house again.

Another year unfulfilled. It's been so long.

She hears sirens and blinks,

trying to touch her nose

with her tongue.

Goodnight silk sky.

Dark. Soft. Good and gone.

VEGETARIAN

I want to take photographs of you sleeping

To place a daffodil bud in your navel

To fall asleep in your lap

On a park bench

In the sun

Atop Parisian soil

I will fill envelopes with your words

TENACIOUS ORBIT

Laboring in lavender and purest cottonwood,

delicate, she pursues your thoughts with the dedication

of an astronomer.

The water faucet whines. Slipping,

soothing bruised and aching lungs in a bath

of scented steam,

       she sighs.

Colors are immediate and only in

photographic shades of gray is she real.

      Photograph: spiraling below dipping willows

           her black white polka dress revolves.

Saturn's rings, millions of miles away,

orphans of ice, outcast debris larger than any city,

glide in concert through bleak ethereal space.

      Perhaps neither are so smooth,

so table-top precise,

grinding, cursing, and clutching for importance and placement,

      schoolchildren shoving for seats on the bus,

or lovers,

      frantically rolling, in moist sheets, like reptiles.

And perhaps,

on not at all a rare occasion,

one crystalline husk splinters, smashed, against another.

There is an explosion.

Pacific disc, calm ease,

a voracious cocktail tray and each hors d'oeuvre breathes,

terrified and being devoured.

Yet beneath this light, in this scented bath

where moments are lifetimes   apart,

the arguments, the fight and shatter of plates,

hurtling of keys and cosmic bodies

are desperate gasps in the night

      where all vast simplicity revolves above, well,

without any ever knowing the distress

and struggle for acceptance

amongst all those that are still and temporarily loved.

SPARK WHEELS & CHALK DUST

Drowning in morning hoarfrost

Truly desperate pleas will glitter,

& so, I've learned how to place little faith in others.

Now don't get me started

Or I'll go on & on about helicopters & search lights,

& our shadows cast upon the bedroom wall.

We were so much bigger!

You were 1, 1 part of me,

As long as we didn't move,

& the lights were never turned off.

Are you able to count on hands & toes

Every sacrifice made?

All those unborn potentials, sons & daughters

Disinfected with soap, bleach, & hot water.

I'm afraid my emotions will be the 1st to die.

Will you marry me?

Your floor is my ceiling, & I think

That says more than it should.

Yes, I believe we did agree

Spark-wheel is an appropriate name,

& on the moon, if you should remove your space-

Suit, you'd die from exposure.

We could always exist there,

As shadows embracing on the bedroom wall.

So, quickly, before you go,

Let me chalk the outline,

& do not get upset with me for laughing.

If you knew — all the while I've waited

For the 1st blossom of spring, only to find it

Patiently awaiting me — you might sigh

& know how, even why,

I've learned to place little faith in others.

YOU SLEEP

The condo

it's elephant-footed

    neighbors' roof

    atop a pull-out couch

a muted TV screen

catches the noise of the world

I focus on the gecko

almost transparent body

how he feels now

everything passing through

him like light

    cats perched like specters.

In her certain mirrors

I cannot see myself

at all.

I am joyous and

breaking down.

The tug over the cliff.

What protects me

is your warmth in the

next room

     that is all, really.

AGAINST THE NIGHT

Here there is nothing

I have taken from you

so I begin with memory

as old Natalie Merchant

songs do

in your condo

against the night

in this placid refrain

where we collect the

fragment

no longer near us

to make ourselves

whole

your bright eyes

in your comfortable home,

the way

you wear your clothes

at night

MAUI CONDO

The geography of this room

I know so well

tonight. I could rise in the

dark   sit at the table

and write without light

your four cats in the dark

I am here on the island

of warm rains

A small condo

        a glass of beer, wood

A small box in the Pacific

        Geckos climb

the walls to peer in

and all day long the tirade

pale blue waves

touch the black shore

of volcanic rock

and falls to pieces here

UNTITLED

You said, *this*

doesn't happen so

quick — and later

so slow.

I must remind you of

someone.

Though I am seduced

by the light from the

ceiling fan and

frantic arguments

near the porch.

I ain't subtle

you run rings

around me

but the quietness

sundress

slim legs

arguing your body

away from me

and I with all the

hunger

I didn't know I had

FISH LADDERS AND LOCKS

The day she left all was gray.

For only a moment

the sun made itself visible, reflecting off the water

of the bay as crumpled aluminum.

Radiating waves of heat and exhaustion,

a coronary sunburst and then gone. The clouds

are smeared wool

without consistency to cling.

I am surrounded by flowers.

Coreopsis Verticillata, miniature yellow

compass-heads as directionless, wild and starry

as the reflection of my eyes lost in yours.

     Purple, violent meadow sage.

Serbian bellflowers hidden in the sunshine

and hinting in the sunset as a honeybee hovers

     tasting the air

thrusting its head like a lion tamer

in a dizzying sexual circus act.

I am wearing your flannel found, and Jon

is with me, but mostly keeps to himself.

When I release him to speak

he says, "Just see it my way,"

and I do.

The salmon splash, forever fooled.

Shredding cotton and splintering through,

the sunlight raps a Morse-code atop the bay,

      and glistens that alien light —

hinting to me.

I'm sure if you were here right now

you say it was talking *at* you.

      A bell sounds in the distance

like a wail, possibly a caw, and I'm fluttering

like a pennant, and you said it feels

like you're dying and need to say so much more.

You'll call.

Kafkian-clouds meta-morph into jellyfish,

snaking tendrils stretch across the sky,

like my sneakers, fishing

and seeking purchase and solid why.

The sun is its own view

and I never can tell if its rising

or climbing.

These fish must be blind, but keep on trying.

I say, *Pitani bwino* because you are leaving.

       I say *Tsalani bwino* because I am staying.

Those two words, by definition

far apart, but so close

on the page.

And you are right. Everything is too brief.

Everything is too eternal and stable and unpredictable.

Bridges salute ornery passenger-stained showboats

forever falling in and out of love.

The Chinook tell me nothing.

Soho don't know.

And the Sockeye, simply angry,

slap and beat themselves pink, as I watch

an elderly couple steer straight and true

into the Lock,

      out of the Lock,

and into the ocean

laughing, lapping them up.

Past the Salt Water Barrier, I alone dive

to test the depth, and how narrow and swift

the ocean becomes a sound

becoming the sea, while above the gulls appear

      placated, nearly bored,

and probably won't mind.

Jon whispers something and I nod in agreement.

At this moment

and in this light

your smile would be luscious and coy.

The waters drift on a whim wind.

I am mesmerized,

understandably silent without purpose,

easing through the carpet-bag memories of you

and I

having come to this.

We are wishing you good luck,

and whispering goodnight. You say it feels

like an episode of *Twilight Zone*,

>   you're dying —

but rather to me

this is just and inevitable and hums.

Perhaps something from Dylan,

whom of which you've become so fond of

somewhere;

a country girl, a heavy weight,

>   a hard rain.

Baby, it's as simple as that, strumming a chord,

you lying flat on my back.

Bwino means good, and the rest

I've left to you. The departure and longing.

Out of a cartoon or a child's crayon drawing,

geese flock, soar in a V.

I suppose I should find beauty

in grace,

or in the unexplained tactical perfection,

or weave a metaphor based on flight

or staying afloat, but I don't you see.

The whole time I thought

Jon was talking about you, but really,

he was talking to me.

So, I'll leave when the sun submits,

yields, swallowed alive

by solar-starved jellyfish. I suppose someone's

feeling shame at a time like this.

I don't you see.

The sun signals with one last wink

before being devoured by the sea. In this hemisphere

its last glimpse wasn't of you but me.

TRIP

What was the name of the town

we drove into and through

    Korean barbeque

    stunned

    brakes lost

having driven our way

up roads

and the mountain-trails

boiling out the cloudy mists

What were the names

we sung though

    my head

wanting to rest on your

thigh

all those miles

of greyness entering the car

      All this

      cloud and stars

but now

under the Pacific night

a star arch of dashboard

the ripe grape moon

we are together

An Apology

I didn't mean to "strangle your kitten."

I didn't mean to lie to you in bed.

I didn't mean the feminist statements.

I didn't mean the "Get-Well" cards,

>   to get our case thrown out of court.

I didn't mean a nice bunch of flowers,

>   "heroic measures."

I didn't mean to give an inch,

>   to beat your sister's arguments to death one time.

I didn't mean to give you completion on the biggest issues of your life,

>   to notice how beautiful, you looked in the dark.

I didn't mean to starve,

>   to feed you.

I didn't mean to let you neglect,

>   to wait on my own so long,

>   to forget.

I didn't mean to kiss you right,

to be so inviting,

to make your mouth suck into a tight little knot.

I didn't mean to pay you.

I didn't mean to be your hostage,

to be your lab rat,

your savior.

I didn't mean for you to be right.

I didn't mean to be a perfect magical miracle,

sacred and unassailable,

to be an angel.

I didn't mean revenge,

to be terrified of losing you,

to be that strong.

I didn't mean for you to ever recover,

to lose control,

to "hand it to you."

I didn't mean to be like God,

to be both curious and cruel.

I didn't mean to be nuts about living with you,

to go through all this trouble,

to be the best story of your life,

to make you choke.

I didn't mean feminist statements.

to lie to you in bed.

to strangle your kitten.

I didn't mean to love you so much, really.